Why Carry the Garbage

How Relational Patterns Cause Problems

Diane S. Carothers

Author's Note

This book, like any book written was several years in the making. It's my first published attempt at writing and I owe a debt of thanks to those who helped: my family, who inspire me but also were a lot of the grist for the mill, as my professor used to say; my colleagues, who I've worked with over the years, both present and past; and the clients who I hope I've helped but who have shown me more about how our inter-relational patterns impact our daily lives. Those patterns start in childhood but can continue to haunt us the rest of our lives if we don't do something to change the nature of them to make them healthier interactions that lead to long lasting successful interpersonal relationships.

Why Carry the Garbage

Table of Contents:

Why Carry the Garbage

Prologue

Do you ever people watch? Most of us do. Do you ever wonder about people's stories? Especially the back story behind what we see or know? As a marriage and family therapist I learn a lot about people's stories. The stories that they remember from the time they were little. The ways their families interacted with each other that made them the people they are today.

We all have a story. We all were born into a family with a mom and a dad. Whether we grew up with them is a different matter. Whether they treated us with love and respect is another thing. Those issues plus the ones we've created on our own in the relationships we've made along the way are the reason folks come in for therapy in the first place.

Something somewhere has gone wrong. Some crisis has become overwhelming. Some burdens have become too hard to handle alone. Something has caused the person to have enough stress in their life that they seek our help. I get to be that person to help. I get to learn their stories. The entire stories of their life because often it's not just the current stressors that are causing issues but some unresolved hurt from the past that has been retriggered by the current situation.

As a Christian I am reminded of the scripture verses in the Bible where it is said that "the sins of the father will carry from one generation to another"[1]. Freud[2] was a therapist who often delved deep into a person's psyche to find out what was causing distress. Freudian therapy is long-term and not for the faint of heart.

Most of us want a quicker fix. But sometimes we do need to look at how we were raised to find out how our thinking was affected that might be causing some of our current stress. That's what this book is about. Patterns in thinking and behaviors. How they get started. How we add to them and create new patterns. The patterns that work for us cause no distress but those patterns that don't work eventually cause things like unhappiness, depression, anxiety, and feeling overwhelmed.

We find ways to cope but sometimes they are not very effective. Sometimes we use drugs or alcohol which never helps but only makes things worse. Sometimes infidelities occur which again only compound problems. Sometimes more subtle forms of addictions take hold like pornography addictions or gambling addictions or shopping addictions. Sometimes we shut down and just refuse to talk to whoever we are in relationship with. Sometimes we talk too much. There are more coping mechanisms out there but these are a few of the big ones.

I have written this using my own life as an example most of the time so that I am not breaking anyone's confidentiality. I pray that those reading this find some answers. I pray that if they see themselves in this situation and the book alone

---

[1]
[2]

doesn't help or scripture alone doesn't help that they seek a competent therapist to help them change those patterns. Change is hard for everyone but well worth the effort. It is possible to make positive changes that will impact future relationships. If I didn't believe that, I couldn't do the work I do. I've seen it happen in my own life.

Chapter 1 The Start of Patterns

How do the dysfunctional patterns get started? We all are born into a family system that has a mom and a dad. So the start of any family dysfunction starts right there. We know from the Bible that the first dysfunctional family was Adam and Eve and that because they ate of the fruit of the forbidden tree they were cast out of the Garden of Eden. This story can be found in the book of Genesis[3].

The Bible is full of dysfunctional family stories. So what is a functional family? One that works well for the most part with few arguments and lots of love and respect to go around. Every child born has a mother and a father. But that's where the similarity ends since there are families who planned to have their baby and ones where the baby was unplanned and possibly not even wanted.

Even planned babies upset the dynamic that the couple had prior to having the baby. Babies are cute but they are also a lot of work and are very demanding to get their needs met. New moms and dads are never quite as prepared as they hoped to be no matter how much planning and preparation they did during the pregnancy. I've heard new parents say they were constantly exhausted and there were

---

times they looked at each other and said, "Why did we do this? And do we want more than one?"

But in most cases everyone survives and the parents adapt to the changes the new baby brings and are really happy they had the baby. Of course there are still those crazy times when they look at each other and ask, "Why?" again just like there are times in any marriage when a couple thinks to themselves, "why did I marry this person who is now driving me crazy?"

In my family, my parents got married because my mom was pregnant with me. So the marriage itself didn't start off on the right foot. My mother was handicapped as a teenager from a roller skating accident that left her with one leg shorter than the other. She returned to high school with braces on her legs and still using crutches. Physical disabilities for anyone make normal dating and relationships difficult at best so I understand how she became sexually active after high school when she was in a relationship.

Too many people equate sex with love and the two couldn't be farther apart. We can have sex with tons of people and love none of them. Think of prostitutes or anyone who doesn't have just one sexual partner at a time. Wives and husbands never understand why their spouse would cheat because they thought they loved each other. Cheating is more about getting some unresolved need met that they feel their current situation isn't meeting or about not being able to control their sexual impulses enough to say no.

It seems women may be more prone to thinking sexual intimacy is emotional intimacy than men, but I've seen men who think once there is a sexual relationship than there is a relationship. Too often people have no clue how relationships even start.

Downton Abbey[4] has been a very popular TV show on PBS that was on for six seasons. It's about a Lord and Lady of the Manor and their staff. It starts out around 1912 so it shows how folks handled relationships in England during that time period. I heard a lot about it and started watching it too and really enjoyed it. As a therapist it was really interesting to see not only male/female relationships but also the relationships between the privileged class and the lower class of servants. It was also very interesting to watch the women's roles and how they progressed over the course of the seasons.

There is something to be learned from the old fashioned courting rituals of past generations. All too often in this day and age people hop into bed with one another without knowing anything about that person at all. Sexual intimacy changes every relationship and if sexual intimacy starts too soon, people get into this false sense of relationship that causes problems right from the get go.

---

[4]

I've seen clients who moved in together within days of knowing each other. They've made babies early on too and then wonder why they are having relationship problems later. They really haven't taken the time to try to get to know that other person before not only becoming intimate but totally entwining each other's lives together. They have no idea whether they are compatible or not. Then they come to counseling for help in repairing a relationship that never started on the right footing.

That's like building a house with no foundation. Just slap some walls together, make it stand up, move in and then when a storm comes and blows it down the people living in it look at each other in wonder at what happened!

Scripture talks about building houses on rock meaning solid ground not on shifting sand[5]. Marriages that last a lifetime are built like that. The couples take time to get to know each other. They even forego sexual intimacy in the beginning until they know each other well enough to take that step. Some even wait until they are married to share sexual intimacy which nowadays is seen as so old-fashioned. During the courtship emotional intimacy is established. Something our current culture seems to understand very little about.

In other cultures there are still arranged marriages. That seems so archaic to us modern folk but maybe there is something to it. Usually the ones arranging the marriages are folks close to the people

[5]

so they know them pretty well and pick out partners based on that knowledge. Of course the arranged marriages that are just for financial gain don't count since those don't really take into account the people but just the financial gain from the union.

My ex-sister-in-law had been married multiple times and was sure she didn't want to meet the man who kept asking about her that her parents told her about. When they did meet, he never left. He was always around to help out. He was a nice man and he was good to her two children. It took some time for him to convince her that he was a good guy since she'd had other bad experiences. But with time, she came around. They are still married to this day. He became the love of her life.

My former husband and I met overseas while in the Army. We talked to each other a lot but really only dated for a little over two months before he asked me to marry him. So it was very fast. We moved in together a few months after our engagement. And a few more months after that we were married. It was about 6 months from the time we met until our wedding. Not really enough time to really get to know someone.

There are marriages that last with short engagements so that isn't always a telling point. It's what happens in that relationship after people are together. Any healthy relationship has to be based on mutual love and respect. There needs to be good communication and healthy ways to resolve issues that come up. And come up they will!

Too often folks got into relationships thinking that other person is going to complete them. That's faulty thinking. While it does feel that if you are with the right person, you are more complete, it's because the relationship itself is healthy that is causing that feeling, not the person. We are made to be in relationship with one another.

But all too soon, in any relationship there is going to be some bump in the road. Someone will get their feelings hurt about something. One partner will say or do something that hurts the other one. It may or may not be intentional. It's how we handle those hurts that start the pattern for that relationship. Now add a baby to the mix

You can see where I'm going. Babies are a lot of work. They wake often wanting to be fed. They need their diapers changed. They are not always on the same schedule as you are. And it takes months for them to sleep through the night. Lack of sleep causes crankiness in the soundest of people. Sometimes babies cry for no apparent reason and neither parent can soothe them. My daughter had to cry daily for an hour for three months until it finally went away. Nothing we did helped. It was like she just needed to cry for an hour.

Everyone has their limits in tolerance. We all have different patience levels. That's why two parents are good because when one parent is spent usually the other one can take over and do what needs to be done. That's what works in healthy families. But dysfunctional families can look very different.

Chapter 2 Growing Up with Negativity and/or Abuse

In healthy families parents can handle the tiredness and the fussiness of the baby. Parents might not always be happy that they had a baby but they can talk about how their expectations of childbirth and being parents were very different from the reality they are living. My daughter's best friend from high school and her husband shared how hard it was for them to transition from just being a couple into being parents. They now have two beautiful children that they love and adore but both of them can talk about the changes the babies made to their lives. They are currently expecting their third child. Communication is the key to a healthy loving relationship.

Most times what happens is the relationship may or may not have been healthy to start with. Now a child is added to the mix which only complicates things further. Parents are tired most of the time and they get snippy with each other. Instead of openly communicating they are yelling and being critical of each other. At some point communication falls apart even further.

Sometimes there was already emotional and/or physical abuse happening in the relationship prior to the children being born. That can carry over to the children. And the price those babies will pay is huge. The results can last a lifetime.

That's why I say a lot of the patterns of how and why we relate the way we do starts in childhood. As we grow those familial relationships create patterns of relating that we take into other relationships. All children learn from their parents who are their first teachers. If children are raised in healthy families they have healthy ways of dealing with issues. If there was dysfunction in the family, their ways of relating may be dysfunctional.

Sometimes people know they come from a dysfunctional family so they are already aware of that. Sometimes they choose a partner with a dysfunction too. That could be because it's what they are used to so it feels normal to them. Or it could be that they do recognize there is a problem but they think they can fix it. That's faulty thinking. It's hard enough to change things in our own lives. We can't change other people to make them who we'd like them to be.

There is a saying that has been floating around for a while now: a woman gets married hoping to change the man while a man marries hoping the woman will never change[6]. Too often that is true. My husband said that I changed after we married. I don't think I did. But I did notice a change in him. He didn't talk to me about things the way we did prior to our wedding. And I had expectations of him helping out more around the house which never really came true.

Expectations are a big problem for lots of people. That's why it's a good idea to really take time to get to know your partner. Everyone has

6

hopes and dreams. That is actually a good thing. We need to have hopes and dreams. If we don't, often we suffer from depression. Hopes and dreams drive us to do our best and become whoever we dream of being. It spurs us to run faster, jump higher, strive harder and achieve the goals we set for ourselves.

If we've grown up in a healthy happy family, we've been imbued with the knowledge that we are loved for who we are. We have healthy self-esteem and we know that with hard work, we can achieve anything and everything we set our minds to.

If we grew up in dysfunctional families we may not have hopes or dreams. Our self-esteem might never have been given a chance to flourish. We might not even love ourselves and everyone needs to love themselves in a healthy way. That means accepting oneself as one is but also striving to always learn and be better.

If we get complacent and content, we might become apathetic about life in general. That apathy might lead to depression. Depression all too frequently has anxiety that comes along side of it. Now we are in a hole we can't see our way out of.

When you meet happy healthy people, they are usually busy people. They enjoy their life. They enjoy their work. They enjoy their family. Of course there might be things in their life at times that go haywire or off track but that doesn't really get them down. Happy healthy people attract other happy healthy people.

That other old saying: misery loves company[7] is all too true too. It seems the dysfunction attracts dysfunction. So sometimes I see folks that you just wonder how or why they ever

---

[7]

were attracted to each other in the first place. We see lots of TV shows and movies where the girl is attracted to the bad boy for some reason. Sometimes that works out but more often than not it doesn't. Nice guys may finish last but I'd rather finish with a nice guy than a not so nice one!

All too often when folks come in for counseling as I start talking to them I find out that their problems come from relationships. It might be from the relationship they are in currently or it might just be from the familial relationships of their childhood that continue to cause them distress.

All relationships take work. It's work to be a couple. It's work to be a parent. And sometimes we don't feel like working on the relationship. That's normal. But most of the time if the relationship is healthy, it's not that much work. Look at any healthy relationships around you and see how they operate. Usually that means they are talking to each other about everyday things and the bigger things too. One doesn't get upset just because the other one is upset. If one partner in the relationship is upset, they can ask the other one if there is anything they can do to help but if not, then it's the person who is upset's job to get out of whatever funk they are in.

Too often we want to blame other people for our problems. Everyone has feelings and everyone gets upset at times. Sometimes we get out of bed upset. Maybe we didn't sleep well or had disturbing dreams. Sometimes we don't always know why we are upset.

My dad was upset a lot when I was growing up. He always seemed to be yelling about something or other. So growing up I heard a lot of yelling. My dad didn't like himself very much. He always felt less than for some reason. He was rejected by the Army for flat feet when everyone was enlisting for WWII. That didn't help his low self-esteem.

He married my mom because she was pregnant and it was the thing people did back in the day. I'm not sure whether they would have married had mom not been pregnant. That didn't bode well for my relationship with him. I found out when I was a young adult that my mom contacted another man first when she found out she was pregnant but that man never called her back. So I always thought my dad always wondered whether I was really his or not. That became more apparent to me when I was a teenager.

I have a sister who is four years younger than I am. We do not look anything alike. She looks like my dad's side of the family while I look more like my mom's side. That also didn't help my dad feel like I was really his.

He had other issues from his childhood that bothered him. Once he commented that he lost his bedroom when his sister married and they moved back in with his family. He said he had to sleep downstairs and use the broom closet for his clothes. That really upset him. He didn't talk much about his childhood except for that one time when he told about losing his room.

People in my family had a hard time getting along with my dad because he tended to think he was right about a lot of things and he would argue the point. No matter what they might have to say, he came across as his answer was the right one. I don't remember him apologizing either if he ever found out he was wrong.

Growing up in that environment had a huge impact on me. Especially once I reached my teens. I only brought a few close friends home and then I hoped that while they were there he didn't get mad about something and start yelling. My close friends knew about how he was because I'd shared that with them. My two best friends also had families with issues. I guess that's why we were friends. When the three of us were together at times we talked about our home lives and how we all wished we'd been born into better families.

One friend's mom had died when she was 8 from epilepsy and her dad had remarried a much younger woman. She didn't live with her dad and stepmom but lived with an aunt and uncle instead. My other friend's parents were older when they had her. They ran a boarding house that was attached to their house. Her mom frequently accused her of having sex with her boyfriend even though they weren't sexually intimate. She used to tell us that she should start having sex since her mom thought she already was anyway.

So those familial patterns that start at birth start affecting us right from birth. We don't really notice them at first. Unless there is physical abuse or sexual abuse, then we might know that something is wrong. But even with those things, many times we don't tell anyone for long periods of time because our abuser threatens to harm us or worse if we do.

But the emotional abuse is by far the most dangerous since it can go unnoticed throughout childhood but it lays the groundwork for the rest of our lives. That old saying: "sticks and stones can break my bones but words will never hurt me"[8] is so untrue. The words do hurt and that sting can last a lifetime.

Growing up in a household that is negative with emotional abuse takes a huge toll on anyone. Healthy self-esteem can't flourish in a household like that. And without healthy self-esteem we are more vulnerable to getting into unhealthy relationships as we grow.

Even folks that grew up in healthy families are vulnerable when it comes to domestic violence. No one goes into a domestic violent relationship voluntarily. Who would? I've seen people who had been in the relationship for up to 4 years before the physical abuse started. Usually some emotional abuse and possibly some addictive behaviors were apparent before that but it takes some time for people to feel comfortable enough to let their true colors come out.

Sometimes violence doesn't come from dysfunctional patterns but is more situational.

8

Maybe life has become overwhelming for some reason. Too many major life stressors happening all at once and no good way to cope with them all and a person cracks. We see that happen too. That can't be predicted but learning how to see red flags in relationships can certainly help to avoid problems.

Chapter 3 Red Flags

So how does one spot the red flags that might make one more vulnerable to a relationship that is not healthy. Unfortunately there is no clear cut way to do that. I have seen so many variations in when relationships have turned sour. Sometimes it starts right from the very beginning because there are two broken people coming together to form a broken relationship. Other times it's not that clear cut and a relationship can look good for a fairly long time before turning bad.

I had a couple once that looked like the dream couple. They were middle aged, attractive, both professionals with good careers. From the outside it looked like they had it all. The wife said they had the dream courtship. They dated for a year when he proposed in the most romantic way that you only read about in romance novels or see in movies. He'd hired a horse drawn carriage to take them to a field where he'd already had laid out a lovely luncheon. This was the place he proposed. Of course she was blown away and said yes! Who wouldn't? Then they were engaged for a year. They moved in together after they were engaged for a year. They lived together for a year before they were married. Keeping track? That's three years of bliss. A year after they married is when things started going south for them.

The husband worked in a family run business. He was the good looking front man for the business but really had little say in day to day operations so the pressure of how he wanted things done and how his family was doing it started to get to him. He started drinking more to cope which started to lead to more arguments at home. One thing lead to another and one time he hit her. That sent her into counseling. Later her husband joined her.

See how his family problems ended up impacting what could have been a beautiful relationship. Unfortunately he'd never broken away from family enough to have his own say in anything and he didn't have a big enough voice in the family to make a difference. Everyone wants to be their own adult at sometime in their life. Family businesses either run very well or have issues because of family drama. So knowing if your partner is involved in some family venture could be a red flag to pay attention to.

Another red flag is if your partner starts to isolate you from your family and friends. This is a huge red flag. When whoever you are dating doesn't want you to have friends or spend time with family, run for the hills! Most abusers isolate their victims from all friends and family. It may start out gradually with giving what sounds like great excuses for why they can't go with you to family events or why they wish you wouldn't go. It sounds innocent enough in the beginning and with the rush of love we feel, we will often give in, in order to please them. We also usually want to spend most of our time with this new love so we don't think too much of it.

What happens over time though is that gradually the connections are gone. Friends stop asking you to do things. Family members become more distant too and get tired of the excuses for why you can't be around. Now couple that with the beginning of self-doubt that starts in because slowly this same partner tears away at your self-esteem.

Again it starts gradually with making comments about not liking you hair or how you are dressed. If you are living together it will be comments about your housekeeping abilities or your cooking abilities. Little negative things at first but then more pointed things that you might actually get angry about. Arguments start to ensue but often they will try to make peace at some point and say they didn't mean what they said. Only they repeat it again very shortly. That starts the self-doubt. You start wondering if they are right.

This partner usually never admits to any wrong doing on their part. Even when you tell them minor things that annoy or might irritate you about them or their behavior, they turn it around to look like it's you, not them. Which again only makes you question yourself. This is emotional abuse and it usually takes place gradually over a long period of time. It can be so subtle that you never know it's happening but you do start feeling more and more unhappy. But now you are isolated too since this partner has cut off family and friends so you have no one but them to talk to about your feelings.

If you try to broach the subject with them they will deny anything of the sort is going on. Which only leads to more self-doubt. This relationship can stay like this for years and years and never change or it can escalate into physical abuse by the partner.

Sometimes the red flags are apparent to one of the people in the relationship but they believe that they can "fix" the other person. So they keep trying to make a broken relationship work that will never work because they are the only ones working and trying. Sometimes it's apparent to family and friends but the abused spouse doesn't really believe them. And they excuse their spouse's behaviors because due to the isolation, family and friends really aren't around them that much to really know what they are like.

Relationships are work. Good relationships have both people in the relationship working to make it a good healthy relationship. There is good open and honest communication and trust. All healthy relationships need trust. They need healthy open and honest communication that continues throughout the course of the relationship.

People don't grow at the same speeds but we all continue to grow and mature. Healthy relationships allow that to happen at each person's timetable. Healthy relationships are not in jeopardy when one person wants to try something new. Their partner will be supportive in that endeavor even though they may or may not want to participate in whatever their partner wants to try.

I was supportive when my husband wanted to open his own business. When I wanted to do the same he was not supportive. He bought me a book and then sat back. That's all the support I got from him and he was pretty clear that was all I was going to get. I was verbally supportive when he started his business. I knew he would be OK at it and that it would succeed. When he'd come home and express concerns, I validated his concerns but offered my encouragement and assurance that I knew he could do it. He did not do that for me. In fact he acted like he didn't even want to hear about what I was thinking.

When I saw problems in our marriage and wanted to talk, he'd shut down. He wouldn't participate in any discussion of what my concerns were or how to make things better. Now that I look back I think that was the change that occurred after we married. The communication that I thought we had prior to our wedding stopped. I kept trying to make it happen but it never was the same again.

I don't know if he was overwhelmed with what he'd done. I don't know if suddenly he felt tied down to one woman. Since he wasn't talking to me I can only speculate. He did tell me after 15 years of marriage that he married me because the time was right for him to marry and if it wasn't me, he would have married some girl soon anyway. Then he listed my attributes that he found attractive: I was good looking enough; I was tall enough and smart enough; and he thought I'd make good babies. I was devastated since he never mentioned love at all. No one should ever marry just because they feel their time for single life is over and that's what the societal norm says they should do. No one should settle for less than what they really hope and dream of in a partner.

Since we were created to be in relationship, we all crave a life partner. Even homosexuals crave a life partner that's why they fought so hard to have the ability to marry. Polygamy and polyamorous relationships don't have a very good track record. We tend to be jealous and don't like sharing. Some folks are fine with living with someone who

24

occasionally has a sexual fling with another person. At least they pretend to be OK with it. I don't know if we were created to be monogamous or not. There is a lot of polygamy in the Bible. Some people are capable of it and some are not. That is something that needs to be worked out in the relationship.

Chapter 4 How to Make Changes

Change is hard. We don't really like change. Some of us are better at it than others. Some folks seem to actually thrive on change and they look for it. They are the adventure seekers, always out trying new things or always learning new things. Most of us though prefer the routines of our life. We do like some adventure that shakes things up a bit and makes life interesting but we prefer knowing what's going to happen.

We go through life thinking we have control over things. That is really kind of funny because anytime any disaster strikes we see that control is just an illusion created by us to make us feel like we have some control. We need to think we have control in order for us not to feel unsettled. It would be hard to live in chaos.

We like that the sun comes up in the morning and goes down at night. We like when the seasons change and we know with some kind of assurity what to expect from the weather. Even though our weather predictions can still be wrong we've learned to predict fairly accurately what is happening.

We may not all believe in global warming but we do know things are changing. We see extinction happen over and over again. We can make note of weather pattern changes. Where I live I notice how things have changed in the years I've lived here. We used to get dense tule fog in the winter that was so thick you could barely see in front of your face. We haven't had fog like that in quite a few years. We may get patches of fog here and there but not for days on end like when I first moved here. Winters are dark and gloomy. But the inability to see through the dense fog is not as bad lately. Is it climate change or the fact that the city is growing so the fog isn't as close to earth as in years past?

So whether we like it or not things change. When we are in relationships, things change there too. I see lots of folks daily with a myriad of issues. Sometimes they come in depressed. I remember one man who came in depressed. He had an affair and as he told his story, he thought he was unhappy with his wife but they had children. The more he talked the more it became apparent that he really didn't like his job.

He'd started a side business that he really enjoyed. As the weeks of treatment went on and we talked more and more, he realized that the marriage wasn't really so bad as the job. He got more and more clients for his side business. His wife even started helping him in the business which meant he started seeing her in a new light. That put a new spin on their relationship.

I never met her. She'd found out about the affair and was able to move past that. When she found out about the affair she took a look at herself and made some changes in her appearance. She lost weight. He shared these things with me. Working alongside her husband had her dressing up a bit. He started seeing her as a professional and not just his wife. They were a good team. They both enjoyed the work.

Eventually he quit his job that he didn't like and started his own company doing what he loved. His wife kept her first job that supplied the family with insurance while she assisted him in his new career. He stopped treatment feeling happy and ready for the new chapter in his life.

When we are unhappy we have to look at what is making us unhappy. Sometimes it's within ourselves. We may say it's the relationship but really we are not happy with the life we've made and need to make some changes. Sometimes those changes seem too hard. Especially when we have a family to help support.

When I moved into private practice I asked licensed therapists who'd been working as licensed therapists for years why they stayed working for the county. They all seemed to have good answers. Kids in college. Spouse died. They wanted the security of the county benefits instead of going it alone. But with that security comes the bureaucracy of working for an agency with all the rules that go along with whatever agency you work for. Sometimes that works out well and other times not so much. Sometimes you get a supervisor who you don't click with. That hampers your ability to do your best if you are at odds all the time. Sometimes when that happens you can change teams or departments but that isn't always an option.

My dad worked as a welder in a foundry. He worked shifts that changed from week to week. He did that all his life. He complained about his job constantly but he never did anything to change it. He thought that was what you were supposed to do.

When I kept changing jobs and going back to school for more degrees he couldn't understand why I would do that.

I've talked with colleagues about ego strength. What gives some people the courage to go out on their own while others never try. That comes from ego strength. The ability to believe in yourself enough to do it even if you fail. It's hard to know how or why some people seem to have it and others don't.

In therapy we talk about holding tanks sometimes. Sometimes the therapist holds things for their clients. We hold their feelings, their hopes, their dreams, their ambitions. We also hold the bad things that are holding them back like the pain, sadness, anxiety, feelings of worthlessness. There are times I've even told clients to leave their garbage or baggage in my office and don't pick it up again.

I worked with a child once who had lots of anxiety. She worried about everything. One session I had her write all her worries down on my whiteboard. She had to leave them there for me to watch over until she came back. When she returned the next week we talked about her week. When I asked about the things she was worried about the previous week, she had forgotten all about them and they no longer were troubling her.

That seems too easy or too trite and yet it works. That's why journaling is such a good tool. You can write your worries down there. You can also write down your hopes and dreams. You can look back later and see if your worries are still a problem for you or if you have made any progress in achieving your hopes and dreams.

A therapist's job is to point out areas where change is possible. It could be in negative thought patterns. It could be in the way one is communicating with their partner. Changes could need to be internal, within one person or more external, meaning in the way we relate to our partner.

Our job is to first point them out and then give possible ways for the change to happen. I can offer a myriad of suggestions but it's still up to the person to make the change happen. Once I get to know people I try to offer solutions that are doable. If the change seems too hard, people won't even try it.

Depressed folks who have suffered with it for a long time have a difficult time changing their negative thought patterns. Folks with anxiety who also have struggled with it for a long time find it hard to do. Change is hard. It takes a lot of effort and work on the person's part who is trying to change.

Chapter 5 Accountability

Maybe one of the reasons we don't like journaling is because then we can look back and see that we aren't making progress. Maybe that's a reason relationships start to fall apart too. When the person we are in relationship with starts to notice that we are all too human and tells us about it, we don't like that. No one likes to see their flaws and yet we all have them. No one is perfect. Everyone fails at times. It's what we do with our failures that matters.

As a child growing up, we have our parents and our teachers and possibly other family members who tell us when we are messing up. All too soon peers also start telling us if we are following the rules or the norms of society or what's expected. That's how we all learn. The biggest lessons are learned by our failings.

Infants learn to walk by falling on their bottoms repeatedly. But they get back up and keep on trying again until they get it. Yet we continue to see failing as something to be avoided. No one likes failing grades and don't think about posting our failings for anyone to see! That's total shame and humiliation!

We really need to see every failing as an opportunity to learn. We learn the most every time we fail. By investigating where we went wrong so we don't make the same mistake over again, we learn to get better. Babies learning how to walk keep working on balance and how to transfer their weight in just the right way so that they don't teeter over. When we learned to ride a bike the principle is the same.

There are lists of famous people who have a lifetime of failures behind them before they found success. Benjamin Franklin[9] had lots of inventions as did Thomas Edison[10]. But how many failures did they each have before their inventions worked? Yet they didn't give up. And that's the secret. Never giving up.

When it comes to relationship though it's a bit trickier. First we need to be able to be open and honest with each other. We need to be able to see

9
10

our own flaws and failings and own up to them. We need to be vulnerable with our partners to be able to communicate about those things so that we can come to some mutual resolution. An accountability partner.

Folks with alcohol addictions who attend AA[11] meetings eventually get a sponsor. That sponsor helps them over the hurdles of alcohol cravings because they've been there. They know what it's like and sometimes they know how to help their sponsee get over the hump and past the cravings. The sponsor becomes their accountability partner. That person who will hold their butt to the fire so to speak, and help them maintain sobriety.

We need to do that in relationships. We need to be each other's accountability partner and be OK with it. When our partner comes to us with some concern or need, we usually want to help resolve it for them since we care about them. If the concern or need is about us though, we may get defensive and then want to fight back rather than be open and honest and admit that there may be an issue there.

We don't really want to change each other, but when we are in relationship we do need to adapt to meet each other's needs. There needs to be mutual respect for each other and acceptance of who each other is as a person. But if something we are doing really bothers another person and we continue to do it in spite of knowing that it's really bothersome for them, that shows a lack of respect. Sometimes we need to adapt and change things just a bit so that both people are still getting their needs met with the least amount of distress for either of them. That's being adaptable and accommodating.

---

[11]

But both people in the relationship need to be doing this.

Communication is vital to make that happen. But it needs to be effective communication that is open and honest and isn't attacking or condemning in any way. And that's often hard. We learn to talk when we are young but no one really teaches us how to communicate effectively. That is unless we take some class, but how many of us do that.

Communication is actually a 6 step process. The first step is the thought one person has. Step two is they say it. Step three, the other person hears it. Step four, they attach their own meaning to what they heard. The final two steps are the crucial ones. The ones we don't do unless taught. Step 5, the hearer repeats back what they thought they heard. That's sometimes called active listening or reflective listening. Step 6, the originator of the message can then either affirm that they heard correctly or say what they wanted to communicate in another way if the hearer took it differently than as it was intended.

Let me give an easy example. Husband comes home from work and his wife informs him that something is wrong with the washer. He repeats back that he understands her to say the washer isn't working right. She tells him that indeed something is going wrong with the washer. Her thought was the washer isn't working I need to let my husband know. So she tells him. He hears it and repeats back what he's heard her say. Now he can ask if she wants him to look at it, call a repairman or what their next step might be.

All too often though it may actually go something like this: the wife tries to do laundry and the washer isn't working. She's now angry and frustrated because she can't get her chores done the way she intended. She lets that simmer inside of her all day. Her husband gets home from a hard day at work and now she explodes at him, "the damn washer isn't working" but doesn't tell him in a nice calm fashion as she's had all day to be frustrated about it. He's equally tired so he yells back, "What do you want me to do about it?" and pretty soon they are in a heated argument over a broken washer.

The washer is broken. She's frustrated. Instead of letting it simmer, she needs to be able to put that aside and do something else and then when her husband gets home, she can calmly let him know the washer is broken so he can say, "OK, what should we do about it?" It's not really news he wants to hear either but sometimes it's the delivery of the news that sets the tone.

Newspapers are great about using a headline to grab our attention. We see it happen all the time. Some kind of hype gets our attention. The news may not even be that great but if the right attention grabbing headline is used, we'll read it or listen to the story.

We do that when communicating with our partners. Most times we are quick, too quick to try to tell our partner something of importance without taking time to think about how we need to deliver the message. Especially if we are tired or hungry or frustrated. In our tiredness or our frustration or feeling hungry, we just want to say what we need to say and move on. Those sometimes are the very times we need to slow down and think about what we are saying and why.

Often times we don't even know why we say what we say to our partner. Especially in the heat of anger. Stupid things get said that can't be taken back. Things that wound and hurt the other person and only make matters worse. Other times we've let things simmer for a while and we know we need to talk about it but we are afraid of how they might react so we keep letting it just simmer under the surface until something upsets the apple cart. Then it all spills out. We bring up issues that happened months or at times, even years ago because they've never truly been resolved.

If we thought of our partner as an accountability partner who was helping us be the best person we can be, it might help. But only if that partner is loving and kind and isn't critical or judgemental when we are less than our best. Therapists often become that person for their clients. Part of my job is to point out errors in thinking or in communicating or behaving but in ways that are helpful. But again the person has to be open to seeing where they might need to make some changes.

One of the problems I often see in relationships is that people do have accountability partners but it's not their spouse. They confide in friends or family members or even a person of the opposite sex. That person then gives them advice or tells them how they see things. When the spouse finds out that their partner has been talking to someone else, most times they get upset. They feel betrayed and like their partner is going outside of the relationship for answers. That starts to erode the trust and all relationships need to have trust to survive.

Sometimes issues in relationships have become so big that outside intervention is necessary but it needs to be with someone competent like a therapist or clergy member. Someone who is impartial and can listen to both parties concerns and try to help them get back on track. Friends and family may be great listeners but they also care about both of the people involved usually, so that puts them in an awkward position of being in the middle. And that can cause more trouble than it's worth.

Chapter 6 Emotional Intimacy

Most couples I see that are having problems do not know how to communicate effectively and they have issues with emotional intimacy. This goes back to what I mentioned earlier about intimacy in general. We are not always good at differentiating emotional intimacy with sexual intimacy. We often confuse sex and love and don't even think about intimacy. When we go from dating to jumping right into bed with someone we haven't taken any time to establish one iota of emotional intimacy.

Emotional intimacy is established over time. It's the time spent getting to know someone on a deeper level. How they think. How they feel. What matters to them in life. What their hopes and dreams are. Where they see themselves in the future. What their belief systems are. Where their moral values lay. Finding out about their work ethic. What kind of person are they in their personal lives. Do they work and are they accountable for their actions. Do they take responsibility when they mess up. Are they trustworthy, reliable, loyal. How do they get along with their family. Do they have friends and how close are they to their friends. What is their educational background. Their cultural and ethnic background. Their religious background.

Truly getting to know someone takes some time. We live in such a fast paced world and we are all too busy and fast paced ourselves in this world that we don't want to take time to get to know another person. Really know them. How well do any of you reading this know your friends? How well do you know your family?

I was informed recently that a distant niece by marriage died of a drug overdose. No one knows if it was intentional or unintentional. My close family didn't know her well at all. We knew some of her story. She'd apparently been molested as a child by a stepfather but which one we don't know as her mother had several husbands. She put herself through college as a stripper. She made headlines in her hometown when she became judge and from all outward appearances her life looked good. It seemed she had overcome the dysfunctional childhood.

But upon closer inspection she was divorced and the reasons were different depending on who you talked to. Her version was her husband cheated. His was she was addicted to prescription pain medication. Both may have been true. And both may have been caused by childhood trauma that was never dealt with. Now her children have to deal with not having her around anymore, with way more questions than they have answers for, which can only impact their future. How is not yet known and has much to do with how they deal with the effects of her death.

I do know that her mother came from a broken home with no fatherly influence from her biological father after her parent's divorce until her mother was a grown adult in her 40's. And even after her mother made contact with her own father their relationship was sketchy at best. He wasn't the kind of father she could go to for advice or even tell anything really relevant to. So that contributed to her own issues with childhood and her early promiscuity. See how the dysfunctional family patterns impact us!

I know some churches are starting programs geared more towards young females on growing up and becoming a woman. Family values are taught in the home. Whether overtly or covertly we are teaching our children what we think and how to act. They watch what we do and what we say. They know if our actions match our words or if we are talking out of both sides of our mouth. That is where our kids start to learn what is expected of them when it comes to relationships in general.

How we interact with our kids is where the patterns start on how they will interact with others. Once kids start daycare/preschool or regular school they start learning how to interact with other adults and peers. Up to that time they are mostly with their parents and extended family where they are learning about interactions. Parents treat their children one way and usually extended family or grandparents and aunts and uncles treat the kids in a different way. That's fine. Kids are adaptable and pretty resilient and they need to have various interactions with various kinds of people in order to learn how the bigger world works.

Kids also learn quickly how to manipulate their parents to get what they want and need. Most parents are pretty good at fulfilling needs but it's the wants that kids will use manipulation on to get their way. Parents need to be on the same page when it comes to parenting issues or the kids can quickly cause all sorts of problems between the parents.

That's where having good emotional intimacy and knowing how to communicate effectively with your spouse is of prime importance. In blended families this becomes doubly important. The kids of one spouse can really sabotage a relationship if the parents haven't fully developed good emotional intimacy and don't have good healthy communication happening.

I've seen so many blended families come in with issues over the kids because prior to marriage the parents didn't really discuss how to raise the kids together. It's hairy enough raising kids after a divorce when the exes don't agree on parenting issues but it makes it worse when the new step-parent has no clue on what is expected of him/her as a parent from the other parent and then they do what they think is right only to have it questioned or overridden causing distress in that relationship.

Now add to that the fact that the kid has multiple adults that are parental figures in their lives. Kids can cause all sorts of issues trying to get their own way. Without good communication between parents, no matter if it's the biological parents or it's the step-parents, the kids get to have a free for all when it comes to being able to cause disturbances in parental relationships.

We've become a society that is so obsessed with child abuse that we are afraid to discipline our kids at times especially after a divorce, because it might be abusive. That other parent then might get full custody of them. That causes fear and distress and so we avoid discipline and the problems get worse and worse.

I will never be out of work. Because we are all human. We all mess up. The best we can do is own our own failures, forgive ourselves, say I'm sorry to those we've hurt and try harder. Being able to do that helps keep the emotional intimacy high.

Chapter 7 Forgiveness

As a Christian we are taught about forgiveness. Forgiveness is an interesting construct to think about. We want to be forgiven for all the mistakes we make and we usually do forgive others eventually for the mistakes they've made. But forgiving ourselves becomes the issue.

Why is it so hard to forgive ourselves? Since I was raised a Christian I tend to look in Scripture for answers to that question. My theory is that I feel so much shame and guilt over messing up, that I feel unforgivable. If that is true, than others can't forgive me either. Right? So my defenses are always on alert especially around those people I've hurt.

I'm checking their comments for forgiveness. Sometimes it's there and other times it's not. When we get upset and frustrated and forget to use our good communication skills, forgiveness is usually not apparent. The words we use when we are upset seem to attack and sting us right where it hurts the most.

Shame and guilt are two very distinct things. Shame comes from the outside. Our parents or other authority figures making us feel less than and that what we've done is so bad that we need to feel shame for it. Guilt comes from the inside. As we grow and learn the difference between right and wrong, we develop our own ability to perceive when we've messed up and we feel guilt.

Neither of these feelings is necessarily bad. I'm not sure anyone grows up without feeling both of them at some time. But as we grow it's how much we feel about either one that can cause issues. Shame really damages self-esteem. If we are constantly shamed we start internalizing that feeling to mean we'll never be able to measure up. Low self-esteem can cause a bunch of issues. We need to have healthy self-esteem. We need to be able to self-correct as needed and feel good about being able to do it. No one is perfect. We all make mistakes. So feeling some guilt at times, helps us self-correct. But shame is more harmful because once we've internalized that feeling, it's very hard to overcome.

Lately I've hurt my mother. It's not been intentional. And every time I try to make it better it just keeps getting worse. So for now I'm not talking to her as much as I was. As we age our patterns of thinking become even more ingrained. It's even harder to change the way we think even if we want to.

I see two kinds of older people: bitter or better. The better ones are the kind ones. Even if they have dementia, they continue to be kind and loving to everyone. The bitter ones are the nasty ones no one wants to be around. As I age I want to be better, not bitter. I want to laugh and not cry. I want to sing and dance a jig, even though it might look pretty funny! And I don't want to fall and break something!

I have been known as the laughing therapist at times because peals of laughter can come out of my office. Not all the time of course. There are tears and anger too. But I try hard to end every session on a positive note. I want my clients to feel better. Not worse. But often things do get worse before they get better. Most folks don't realize that, so at times I need to actually tell them that.

We like stability. We hate change. Change can be both good and bad. Life is all about changes. We've learned to live with some with minimal frustration but others continue to bug us. If we're having a bad day, even the weather can tick us off.

Forgiveness has to be a given in all relationships. We are quick to forgive the small things. We are quick to forgive almost everything when a relationship first starts. Then we are "in love" with our partner, the newborn, our new best friend... But all too soon, the reality that our partner has flaws and sometimes forgets about us. Babies poop and cry and... And even our new best friend doesn't always seem to be honest all the time. The love matures into a deeper more mature type of love. One that encompasses understanding of what that other person might be going through.

Most problems with spouses or long-term relationships come from the untold expectations. The gender roles each one assumes the other will fulfill. Those are usually determined by the family we were raised in. For instance, mom cooks, cleans, does laundry. Dad mows the lawn and takes care of the car and house. Girly things for girls and manly things for boys. Very stereotypical.

Problem is we live in 2017 so gender stereotypes don't work well any longer. Usually both parents are working outside of the home. We want to share responsibilities and duties. But how often do we talk about that? Especially prior to marriage or cohabitating? And even if we do talk about it, talking and actually living together are often too very different things.

So we move in together and at first the cap off the toothpaste or the raised toilet seat is amusing. Then we go to the bathroom in the middle of the night and fall in! Not too funny now. The toothpaste is dried out every stinking day. Not funny. So the minor irritations of just getting used to living together fade the romance pretty quickly.

If there are kids in the mix, that only compounds the problems even faster. Kids are the same now and forever. They want to explore. They get into things. They can be noisy and messy. We have our own style of disciplining that may or may not work, but we try. And depending on the age of the child, some come with attitudes! Forgiveness is needed more than ever! Sometimes multiple times in a day. Especially during those teen years!

Every parent knows what I'm talking about. When they are little it's cute but even little ones get on our last nerve at times. When they are teens, the attitudes can cause major havoc. Teens can kill a blended family. But so can younger kids or even adult children if the couple lets them. None of us would have survived if our parents didn't know how to forgive us!

In relationship we also need to be able to hear the other person's perspective on things. We are not the same person. We are two very distinct people with each having their own thoughts and perceptions of events. Being able to see things from the other person's perspective is very helpful. That doesn't mean we always agree. It just means we are trying to understand how they view the world. Some folks can do this and others are so used to seeing things their way and getting their own way, that even attempting to see things from another view is difficult. That can cause major problems in a relationship.

I have a couple I'm working with now who have been married for a long time. The husband got very negative at home primarily due to a nasty work environment. But he'd also been raised in a family that was more negative than positive. So home life had been pretty miserable for a while because he brought all his work tensions home.

His wife was an introvert. That made it harder for her to communicate any of her thoughts and feelings to him. She would try at times to let little hints out but he wasn't good at getting her hints. He said his family was always straight forward and just said what they needed to say. He was not introverted so he had no understanding of how his wife communicated.

As their marriage progressed the wife got really good at reading when her husband was distressed. She had her own way of trying to leave him alone or trying to be kind to help alleviate his stress. Because she was an introvert, being alone was her way of getting her head back together. So frequently that was the way she dealt with his dark moods.

Since he wasn't an introvert, he craved the company of his wife. But he had a hard time letting go of the negativity which came out at home as criticism about anything and everything. That made her even more reticent to bring up things to him.

He wasn't a yeller but he wanted to always be right. Even in sessions it became apparent that he

43

used questioning and comments as ways to keep the conversation going, hoping to win the other over to his way of thinking. That became even more tiresome for her since communication had never been her strong suit.

Over the years she spent more and more time doing things she enjoyed to the exclusion of her husband until she reached a point where she couldn't take it anymore and asked him to move out. That's where they were when they started counseling. Change has been very hard for this couple. The husband has a harder time than his wife, mainly because she's done a of lot of her own introspective work over the years. He didn't have a clue what was happening in their relationship because even when she attempted to talk to him and let off some steam, he couldn't see his part of the problem and always turned it back on her and then kept at her, trying to get her to agree with him until she'd stop talking.

Sometimes our patterns become so entrenched that it's like a battleground. And no one is willing to concede. I often tell couples that there are no winners in a marital argument. Only losers with both of them losing if they aren't able to see the other person's perspective on things. Again that doesn't mean we must be in agreement. We can choose to disagree and leave it at that. But we do need to accept that as an option. And we do need to be able to forgive each others faults for being human.

So we are back to why it's so hard in relationships to forgive each other. The answer is as simple as it is complex. We don't like admitting we have flaws and we certainly don't like it when someone else points it out. It's even worse when it's the person we love! Remember, we hid all those nasty flaws during courtship. Now they are exposed and out in the open for the other person to see and we are ashamed and embarrassed.

OK, just own it. That's easy. Right? Easier for some than others. My mother doesn't own most of what she's done. And it seems to be getting worse the older she gets. Poor pitiful mom. She's very good at shaming and blaming. As I think back over my childhood, I'm not sure I ever heard my mom say she made any mistakes. She didn't act like she was perfect but she didn't really own up to mistakes she'd made either. I do own my mistakes and have for a very long time.

Shaming is one of the worst abuses. It makes us feel worthless, less than, like we should have never been born at times. At it's worse it can lead to suicide. Yet we are all guilty of it. Shame gets things done at times. Other times it leads to addictions. If I'm as messed up as people tell me I am, I want to escape from that in some way, shape, or form. Drugs, alcohol, gambling, sex, pornography, shopping, food... Name the addiction and someone has tried it and still is trying it.

Escape doesn't work. Robin Williams lost his battle. He was brilliant and yet he succumbed to whatever shame he felt and however worthless he felt. Suicide isn't an answer. It leaves way more questions for all those that loved the one gone. Then they start the shame game on themselves. The if only's. The should have, would have, could have...

One client told me his brother had an accident. He'd committed suicide. I believe that client. As a therapist I know if I can get a client past that moment of suicidal ideation, it will pass. It may return, but for the moment they are in a safe place.

They are safe in my office. If I can help reframe their negative self-talk into more positive, maybe I can stave off the suicidal ideation for a little longer.

I've only lost one client that I'm aware of so far. And I'm not sure it was suicide. He was angry and driving through a canyon that drops off on one side. He went over the side. Did he do it purposefully? Or was it an accident? I will never know. No one will because folks that drive too fast go off the side of that canyon frequently. Did I look over my notes, especially the more recent session notes? Of course I did. He was in a good place. He'd made a decision to leave his wife. He was feeling hopeful and confident that he could move on. And I hadn't seen him in months.

What happened? Maybe his wife could tell. She's the one who called our office. All she said was he was dead. I had to read the newspaper obituary to find out more and that was sketchy. Just another car that went off the canyon. I'm sorry it happened to him. To Robin Williams. To the brother of my client. To anyone. Forgiveness. It's crucial.

But forgiveness of ourselves is as important as forgiveness of others. If we can't forgive ourselves of the dumb things we've done, we will add to the problems in our relationships. Everyone needs to own their own part of the problem. That's hard to do. It's hard to be vulnerable. Especially with those we love. They could use that against us and often do when the next argument arises.

So learning how to forgive each other and ourselves becomes part of what happens in treatment. Always remember, there are no winners and losers in an argument with those you love. Only losers. No one is always right and no one is always wrong. No one is better than the other. Both parties have feelings that can be hurt.

And forgiveness doesn't mean forgetting. We aren't supposed to forget but learn from everything we've been through. If we forget we are prone to repeat our mistakes. Look at history. So while forgiveness is crucial forgetting will not happen. What will happen is that the bad memories will fade and be replaced by new better memories.

Chapter 8 Maintaining Positive Changes

OK, so how do folks maintain the positive changes they make during treatment? Let's go back to that accountability partner. Find a close friend, not your partner, who will tell you when you are being snarky or too overbearing or... Your partner can also point out that the changes seem to be slipping away.

That has to be done very carefully though. Using those "I" statements you learned to use, or it will end up back in another argument. I have a repeat client currently who I treated just several months ago. We did couples therapy. She came alone and said that she was a repeat. We joked about needing a "tune up".

Her husband works in law enforcement and with all the media headlines lately about cops being killers because they respond too quickly, he's been stressed. Didn't help that the local police made national news over just that recently either. I had to remind her of that.

But she was spinning out of control with worry that they'd lost all the headway they'd gained when I saw them months ago. I had to keep reeling her back in and keep reminding her that things are not as dark as she thinks. It took almost the entire session to get her anxiety to calm down.

Our best work is often done in the last few minutes. That's when they really settle in and can hear what you might be saying. I wish sessions could be longer at times. And then again I don't because I'd still spend the same amount of time calming fears and it would still just be the last few minutes where they would calm enough to take something home with them.

Have you ever tried to change your signature? I'm older so we had to learn cursive and penmanship was something we were graded on in school. I remember as a teen I changed the dots over the letter i to a heart shape. It was an intentional change on my part but it still caught me off guard at times and I would just use a dot.

I sign my name so many times over the course of a day and yet my name is legible. I worked as a respiratory therapist. I had to decipher the doctor's notes. It was pure decoding at times. That can be dangerous when you can't decipher what meds to use! I got really good at it. Even my worst signature is legible.

That is something simple. Just think how hard it becomes to change a pattern that has been in place since childhood! And most of our patterns stem that far back. I always do a pretty complete intake at the first session. I want to know about medical issues, surgeries, and gynecological health. I ask about your sex life, your sleeping patterns, what allergies you may have and what meds you are on. I ask about illegal drugs, alcohol use, cigarette use.

Our bodies are physical but we also have emotions. So if we are unwell, we are going to be testier and more irritable. We are spiritual beings no matter what religion you believe in or whether you believe at all. Everyone believes in something. Hope keeps us going. We are sexual beings. We were made to have sex and enjoy it. Not just procreate. We are some of the only animals who have sex just for fun.

I need to look at the whole person. Then I can start looking at the relationships that are causing them problems. I ask about their childhood. Was there abuse and what kind. How many times have they been married or in a long-term relationship. I ask teens if they are sexually active, usually after their parents leave the room so as not to divulge their confidence in me.

Confidentiality is crucial in the therapeutic relationship but it's even more crucial in a loving relationship. Telling the others faults to friends and families only inflames the problem. It never solves it. Now you've got the whole darn family involved in your personal drama. That's what soap operas are for!

Families that are overly involved we call enmeshed. Every family member knows every other family members business. The grapevine is alive and well, thank you very much. Much to the chagrin of at least one of the people in the relationship.

I remember my mother sharing with my grandparents that they found my birth control when I was in college. Fortunately my grandparents never said a word to me about it! They were awesome and loved me unconditionally. But my mother was hoping that if they did say something, I'd stop having sex. Once that genie has been opened, there is no going back!

She was not happy with my snappy comeback that at least I wasn't going to get pregnant! Both of my male cousins got girls pregnant while they were in high school. Both married the girls. Both divorced them. I thought I was being smart about it.

So change is hard to maintain. But healthy relationships learn how to do it. What makes me sad is when I ask clients if they know anyone who has a long term relationship and their answer is no. That tells me a lot about not only their family dynamics but also their friend base.

My grandparents married in their 50's after both of their first marriages failed. That was not well publicized back in the day. You didn't share that you were divorced. It was a huge failure, especially if you were believers. They were my role models as a child.

My grandmother was 72 when she died and my grandfather missed her until the day he died 12 years later. He dated as an old man, even younger women, but no one could ever replace my grandmother. She was his true love. And he was hers. I wanted that too.

Sometimes we get lucky and our first marriage is that. Sometimes we get lucky on a second or third try but each try makes the odds less likely. I know I probably will not ever be married again. And that's OK. I share lots of husbands of all ages with my friends. That's OK too since I keep very healthy boundaries and would never cheat! I love and respect my friends too much for that.

Once one divorces, it's much easier to kick the next partner to the curb rather than try. We've already done it once. It's quite expensive but everyone knows people who've been married multiple times. Look at the movie stars. Some even marry the same person more than once! Guess they hope the second time might be better.

We do mellow with age some so maybe it will. But remember, I said as we age we either get better or bitter. I would never take my ex back. He's getting more and more bitter. He's even more of a misogynist than he was before. He makes racial remarks at times and he wasn't really racist. My son said he can hardly stand to be around him for very long at times when he's in one of those moods. That's sad.

I want my kids to want to be around me. I want to laugh and play. I want to be the biggest loser when we play games together. I want to go shop with them. And vacation with them. We truly enjoy each other's company most of the time.

It's not the same with all my kids though. My relationship with my oldest son is more strained than with the younger two. If he's alone, he's a jewel and we can have nice talks. But if anyone else is around, he has to behave differently depending on who's there. Part of that is to hide his own issues. He suffers from PTSD from the wars he's been in serving in the Army. Another part is learned from his dad.

You see his dad couldn't share real feelings. He learned at a young age if he did he would get told why that wasn't appropriate. Mostly by his mom. She told both of her children what she wanted them to be when they grew up. Neither of them did what she expected. Each acted out in their own way.

51

My ex got really good at hiding feelings deep down inside.

Change is hard. But it is well worth it. At any age but the sooner it can happen, the better because hopefully the changes will have more of a chance of becoming the normal way of relating.

<u>Chapter 9 Worth the Effort</u>

So now you may be asking whether it's worth the effort. I can't answer that question anymore than I can answer whether someone should stay together or not. Of course if there is abuse that is physical or sexual they need to get out of that relationship. Emotional abuse is a harder one to determine. What's abuse to one person is not to another.

That goes back to their family of origin too. If they were raised in an emotionally abusive household, they are already used to emotional abuse. All too often abused folks end up with other abused folks. It's almost as if there is some magnetic attraction of some kind.

More likely it's because they've become accustomed to those patterns of behaviors so they feel right to them. I have a new couple I'm working with. The wife was raised by a single mom for many years because her parents had never married and mom had left dad years ago when she was young. Her mom did remarry but dominated her stepdad. Mom ruled the roost. So wife rules the house. That works for some things and not so well for others.

Husband had a distant mom who was never really there for him. Dad was in prison so he was not really attached to dad. While he appreciates his wife taking charge, he often feels put down and like what he does contribute isn't appreciated because in her domineering, she's often critical and negative.

Currently they are living apart but they have two young children. I am a firm believer that if they really want to change, they can. Wife kept asking me for guarantees. I had to tell her there are no guarantees. Not in life. Life isn't fair and never has been. Get over that thought. But with hard work, they can make their marriage stronger than ever.

This was only their second session and her husband wasn't in the first one. The work is up to them. It always is. Love is a choice. We wake up daily and choose to be happy or sad. We choose to love our mate and our children. Some days those choices seem easy. Some days they are hard. Some days we may choose to hate those we love and other days we may love them but hate the way they behave at times. The opposite of love isn't hate. It's indifference.

Indifference. Lack of caring. Not giving one iota what is going on with the other person. Once you've been in a relationship with someone, not caring anymore isn't an option. I was married for 20 years. We had three kids together. There is a part of my heart that my ex will always have, forever.

Most of the time now, I feel sorry for him. Exchanging spouses doesn't always work out well. And it definitely hasn't for him. He's become old and bitter. His wife is sick and on a lot of medication. Being married to him doesn't help her. He's a horrible caregiver.

So I can't guarantee any fixes for anyone I treat. That's on the people I work with. My college professor told us that as therapists if we are working harder than our clients, something is wrong. They come to us for help. Help we give. But the work is theirs to do. I can reframe negative thought patterns, but it's their job to start doing that for themselves.

I can teach better ways to communicate, but again they have to put it into practice. Practice makes perfect. But only perfect practice makes perfect. Imperfect practice doesn't help. It has to be a conscious concerted effort on their part to make positive changes in their own lives. Each person individually.

I read an article recently that someone wrote about things we need to make a relationship work. The person writing it talked about marriage being a covenant relationship.[12] But we want to think of it more as a contract where things should be 50/50. The term covenant is not readily used except in religious contexts so most of folks may not even know what that means. As a Christian a covenant is a promise made with God so the marriage covenant is a promise both people make with God when they take their marriage vows. But not all people are married in the church.

And most people, even if they are married in the church, don't realize how sacred that vow is meant to be. They don't even think about their marriage being a commitment. Sometimes they don't realize the vows they've said to each other. At other times they don't like the standard wedding vows so they write their own.

---

[12]

Then there are those folks who don't get married in a church but have civil ceremonies. Almost anyone can go online and become certified to marry others. And there are those folks who form a relationship, move in together and have children with no formal ceremony of any kind. There might not even be a talk about commitment or what moving in together entails prior to their doing it.

California is not a common law state that recognizes cohabitation even if couples have lived together for years. That's why we heard of palimony cases years ago. Divorce is costly, both financially and emotionally. People rush into relationships with no regard for the long term until things go sideways. Then suddenly they want to split up but that is not an easy or pain free process.

So this article talked about thinking of marriage not as a contract but as a covenant. With both people in it 100/100. In the beginning of all relationships we tend to put the other person first. But there is a subtle change that takes place once we've been in relationship for a while. Suddenly it's not so comfortable to always put our partner's needs ahead of our own. We are human and we also have wants and needs. But if both parties continued to do that and overlook petty differences, marriages would be a whole lot happier and smoother.

If we were sure to give 100 percent all the time and so was our partner, what a difference that would make. But kids need 100 percent too. And we are each just one person. We get tired. We are not always on our best game. Sickness comes. Nerves get raw. And we can't be nice 100 percent of the time.

If we remember that we married for life and there is no easy out, it helps since we have to find a way to get over our stuff and move on. Also we need to be able to express discontent in a way that's not harmful to the other person. Using "I" statements so we are owning our own thoughts and feelings and remembering those six steps of communication helps. So does never name calling or saying hateful hurtful things just because we are upset.

Everyone gets angry and frustrated. It's just a mood that passes. It's what is said and done when we are in that mood that leaves lasting marks. If we try to be respectful even when we are at our worst, this too shall pass and we move back into a more happy harmonious relationship.

Being able to not internalize each other's stuff is important too. Who owns the problem? Can the partner help or is it just one person's problem to deal with on their own. We can validate feelings and be supportive but we can't always solve each other's problems. Knowing who owns it and how to just be a supportive spouse is important. I've had clients who take everything personally. They are always upset because someone in their sphere is upset. Could be family but sometimes they extend that to coworkers and even strangers because their need to please is so great that they've learned to make everyone else's problems their own.

Those people live very distressful lives that take a toll on them eventually. Those people learned very early in childhood that they were the cause of every bad thing that happened in their lives. How did they come to this? There are many possible causes but at some point when they were young, they got blamed for everything. They were never praised or told they did things right so at some point they believed they could only do wrong things and everything was their fault. As adults they are still people pleasers. Trying desperately to please everyone around them. And that is not ever possible.

Everyone needs praise and to know they have self-worth. Everyone deserves to be loved. Sometimes families have so much distress in their lives there is no room to show love or praise. People are just too busy surviving. Other times there is just too much violence of one kind or another. Or there is addiction to drugs or alcohol.

I have a mobile that hangs in my office. I use it to represent a family system. When the heat or air turns on, it moves a little. When I am demonstrating for clients what it represents, I pull on a ribbon and the whole thing bounces. That shows that just one person can change the whole family dynamic.

But change is hard. I can't change the family dynamic in my family of origin, because as my mom just told me this morning, she doesn't want to change. She is set in her negative patterns and thinks she's too old for change. I have changed too much for them. Currently I can't even email my mom daily because "I analyze them too much". Her words.

The problem with being a professional of any kind is that role takes over and we can't stop being who we are. When I taught, I was teaching everywhere. I still teach clients things daily. I've been a therapist for quite a few years now so analyzing people is as natural to me as breathing. I don't mean to analyze my family. It just happens.

I've had my own counseling. And in the course of that counseling I know why I was the way I was. I made a very conscious effort to change over the years. None of my family has ever been to counseling. They don't see the need and can't afford it. So nothing has changed for them except what time has forced. So for now, I am not emailing my mom every day.

She won't understand any explanations I try to give. It only makes things worse and she internalizes it all. She still doesn't see that she's being critical of me when she tells me "you are going to send me to my grave with a broken heart". So I have to forego daily emails. My mom is 87 and in relatively good health for her age.

I will email but I will have to keep it light and not bring up anything negative. I can't turn her grumbles and complaints into anything positive because she sees that as me trying to "fix" her. I will have to be very intentional in my emails when I do email her.

Eventually I'll mess up and tick her off. If I don't email for a while, she always initiates a conversation. Usually it's still negative but since I've stopped the daily emails, it's not as negative as it's been so some part of my message to her got through. That's who she is. That's who my sister is. I can't change them. I have to love and accept them just as they are.

Is it worth it? I would feel really guilty if my mom died and we were at odds. I would know why but it would make the loss even more painful. Only you can decide if the changes you make are worth it.

Change takes time. It takes practice. It takes patience. But I believe with everything that is in me, that's it's more than worth the effort. I couldn't work in my field if I didn't believe that. Keep working the positive changes! And if you can't make changes on your own, please find a competent therapist to help you. If one therapist doesn't work, find another. We have personalities too and sometimes our styles don't mesh with who you are. You need to find the right therapist for you. One that listens and understands and gives you insight into the patterns that might be affecting your relationships.

Change is worth it. You are worth it. You owe it to yourself!

End Notes

Prologue

1. Exodus 34:7, Deuteronomy 5:9
2. Sigmund Freud, Psychoanalyst, May 6, 1856-September 23, 1939

Chapter 1

3. Genesis 2:7-3:24
4. Downton Abbey – historical period drama created by Julian Fellowes for ITV in the United Kingdom airing first September 26, 2010.

5. Matthew 7:24-27

Chapter 2

6. H. M. Harwood, "Cynara", 1930

7. Attributed possibly to Christopher Marlowe in his play "Doctor Faustus", 1604 and also sometimes to Henry David Thoreau. July 12, 1817-May 6, 1862.

8. Earliest citation from American Periodical, The Christian Recorder, March 1862.

Chapter 5

9. Benjamin Franklin, January 17, 1706-April 17, 1790.

10. Thomas Edison, February 11, 1847-October 18, 1931.

11. Alcoholics Anonymous founded in 1935 by Bill Wilson and Dr. Bob Smith in Akron, Ohio.

Chapter 9

12. Covenant – Biblical definition means a formal alliance made by God with His people.

www.ingramcontent.com/pod-product-compliance
Lightning Source LLC
Chambersburg PA
CBHW070618290526
45790CB00002B/934